AF661262

Soft Skills for Professional Excellence

CONTENT VIBES
PUBLISHERS • PRINTERS • AGGREGATORS

Soft Skills for Professional Excellence

Pankaj Kumar Ojha
Assistant Professor
Department of Agricultural Extension
Banda University of Agriculture & Technology
Banda Uttar Pradesh

Pragya Ojha
Subject Matter Specialist (Home Science)
Krishi Vigyan Kendra
Banda Uttar Pradesh

CV CONTENT VIBES
PUBLISHERS • PRINTERS • AGGREGATORS

CONTENT VIBES
PUBLISHERS • PRINTERS • AGGREGATORS

1168, Sector 13, Urban Estate
Karnal-132 001, Haryana
Tel: 91-84470 75807, 18440 41168
Email: contentvibesppa@gmail.com
www.contentvibes.in

Print ISBN: 978-93-67551-63-9
ebooks-ISBN: 978-93-67554-03-6

Preface

This book offers a foundational guide to the essential soft skills required for success in both professional and academic environments. Focused on practical development, the books covers covers six core competencies: Effective Communication, Teamwork and Collaboration, Problem-Solving, Time Management, Adaptability, and Emotional Intelligence (EQ).

Each chapter explores the theoretical principles behind the skill, followed by real-life applications, reflective exercises, and strategies for improvement. Emphasis is placed on interpersonal dynamics, resilience in changing environments, and self-awareness—all of which are vital in the modern workplace. The book is ideal for students, early-career professionals, and anyone looking to enhance their employability and leadership potential.

Authors

Contents

1

Effective Communication

Objective: Equip participants with the skills to communicate clearly, confidently, and empathetically in verbal, non-verbal, and written forms to foster collaboration, reduce misunderstandings, and build stronger workplace relationships.

Why It Matters

Effective communication is the cornerstone of professional success. It ensures ideas are conveyed clearly, builds trust, and prevents conflicts. Poor communication can lead to misaligned expectations, decreased productivity, and strained relationships. For example, a vague email can cause project delays, or a misunderstood tone in a meeting can create tension. This module empowers participants to master communication in diverse workplace scenarios.

Learning Outcomes: By the end of this module, participants will:

1. Understand the components of effective communication (verbal, non-verbal, written).
2. Practice active listening and empathetic responses to enhance interpersonal connections.
3. Craft clear, professional written messages tailored to their audience.
4. Apply communication strategies in real-world scenarios through interactive exercises.

Key Concepts

1. Verbal Communication

Verbal communication involves spoken words and how they are delivered. It's not just about what you say but how you say it. Key elements include clarity, tone, and audience awareness.

- Clarity and Conciseness: Use simple, direct language to avoid confusion. For example, instead of saying, "We might potentially consider reallocating resources," say, "We plan to reallocate resources next week."

- Tone and Delivery: Adapt your tone to the context (e.g., authoritative for presentations, collaborative for team discussions). A warm, approachable tone fosters trust, while a harsh tone can alienate colleagues.
- Active Listening: Listening is as critical as speaking. Show engagement by paraphrasing, asking questions, and avoiding interruptions. For instance, if a colleague says, "I'm overwhelmed with this project," respond with, "It sounds like you're feeling stretched. Can you share what's most challenging?"

Illustration Idea

Create a slide showing a "Verbal Communication Triangle":

- Clarity (base): A speech bubble with "Clear, concise words."
- Tone (left side): A smiling face next to a shouting face, labelled "Warm vs. Harsh."
- Listening (right side): An ear with arrows pointing to a brain, labeled "Understand, Reflect, Respond."
- Include a caption: "All three elements must align for effective verbal communication."

2. Non-Verbal Communication

Non-verbal cues (body language, facial expressions, gestures) often convey more than words. Research suggests up to 55% of communication is non-verbal (Mehrabian, 1971). Misaligned non-verbal signals can undermine your message.

- Eye Contact: Maintain steady (but not intense) eye contact to show confidence and engagement. For example, when presenting, scan the room to connect with all audience members.
- Body Language: Use open postures (e.g., uncrossed arms, leaning slightly forward) to signal approachability. Avoid defensive postures like crossed arms or turning away.
- Facial Expressions: Match your expressions to your message. A smile conveys warmth during casual conversations, while a neutral expression is better for serious discussions.
- Cultural Sensitivity: Be aware of cultural differences. For instance, prolonged eye contact may be respectful in some cultures but uncomfortable in others.

Illustration Idea

Design a "Body Language Do's and Don'ts" chart:

- Do's: A person standing with open arms, smiling, making eye contact (labeled "Engaged, Approachable").
- Don'ts: A person with crossed arms, looking down, frowning (labeled "Closed, Disengaged"). Add a note: "Your body speaks louder than your words—ensure alignment."

3. Written Communication

Written communication (emails, reports, instant messages) requires precision and professionalism, as there's no tone or body language to clarify intent. Poorly written messages can lead to confusion or misinterpretation.

- Structure: Use a clear format: subject line (specific), greeting (personalized), body (concise), and call-to-action (e.g., "Please confirm by Friday").
- Audience Adaptation: Tailor your language to the recipient. For example, use formal language for clients ("Dear Ms. Smith") and conversational language for colleagues ("Hi John").
- Proofreading: Check for grammar, spelling, and tone errors. A single typo can undermine credibility.
- Tone Awareness: Avoid overly blunt or emotional language. Instead of "You missed the deadline," write, "I noticed the report is still pending. Can we discuss a new timeline?"

Illustration Idea

Show a "Before and After Email" example:

- Before: Subject: "Stuff"; Body: "Hey, u need to send the report soon, k?" (Labeled "Vague, Unprofessional").
- After: Subject: "Action Required: Q2 Report by Friday"; Body: "Hi Sarah, Please send the Q2 report by Friday, April 25. Let me know if you need support. Best, Alex" (Labeled "Clear, Professional").
- Include a checklist: "Subject, Greeting, Purpose, Action, Sign-Off."

Activities

Activity 1: Active Listening Role-Play

Objective: Practice active listening to build empathy and understanding. Setup: Pair participants; provide a handout with instructions.

Instructions

1. Step 1 (5 minutes): Person A shares a work-related challenge (e.g., "I'm struggling to balance multiple deadlines"). Person B listens without interrupting, using non-verbal cues (nodding, eye contact) to show engagement.
2. Step 2 (3 minutes): Person B summarizes what they heard (e.g., "It sounds like you're feeling overwhelmed because you're juggling several tasks. Is that right?") and asks one clarifying question (e.g., "Which task is most urgent?").
3. Step 3 (5 minutes): Switch roles and repeat.
4. Debrief (7 minutes): As a group, discuss:
    - How did it feel to be truly listened to?
    - What barriers (e.g., distractions, urge to interrupt) arose?
    - How can active listening improve workplace relationships?

Facilitator Tips

- Circulate to ensure pairs stay on task.
- Encourage Person B to avoid giving advice—focus on listening.
- Use a timer to keep the activity on track.
- Illustration: Include a handout with a "Listening Checklist":
- Maintain eye contact.
- Nod or use small affirmations ("I see").
- Paraphrase to confirm understanding.
- Ask open-ended questions.

Activity 2: Email Rewrite Challenge

Objective: Enhance written communication by transforming vague or unprofessional messages into clear, actionable ones.

Setup: Provide participants with a printed or digital copy of a poorly written email (see below). Prepare a whiteboard or slide for group sharing.

Sample Poor Email:

Subject: Update

"Hey team, we gotta do the thing soon. It's kinda urgent. Thx."

Instructions

1. Step 1 (5 minutes): Individually, rewrite the email to make it clear, professional, and audience-appropriate. Encourage participants to include a specific subject, greeting, purpose, and call-to-action.

2. Step 2 (5 minutes): In pairs, share and critique each other's rewrites. Focus on clarity, tone, and structure.
3. Step 3 (5 minutes): Select 2-3 participants to share their rewrites with the group. Facilitator writes key improvements on the whiteboard (e.g., "Added deadline," "Used polite tone").

Sample Improved Email

Subject: Action Required: Project Plan Submission by April 20
"Hi Team, Please submit your project plans by end of day Monday, April 20, to ensure we meet our client deadline. Let me know if you need clarification or support.

Best regards,

[Your Name]"

Debrief Questions

- What changes made the email more effective?
- How can you apply these principles to your daily emails?
- What challenges do you face in written communication?

Facilitator Tips

- Provide a template for participants who struggle (e.g., Subject, Greeting, Body, Action, Sign-Off).
- Highlight real-world consequences of poor emails (e.g., missed deadlines, frustrated recipients).

  Illustration: Create a slide comparing the poor email and improved email side by side, with annotations highlighting improvements (e.g., "Specific subject clarifies urgency," "Call-to-action sets expectations").

Activity 3: Non-Verbal Communication Observation (15 minutes)

Objective: Increase awareness of non-verbal cues and their impact on communication.

Setup: Arrange participants in a circle or small groups. Prepare a short script (see below) for volunteers to act out.

Script Example

- Scenario: A manager giving feedback to an employee.
- Volunteer 1 (Manager): "I'm really impressed with your recent work, but I'd like you to focus more on meeting deadlines."
- Volunteer 2 (Employee): "Thanks for the feedback. I'll work on that."

Instructions

1. Step 1 (5 minutes): Two volunteers act out the script twice:
   - First time: Manager uses positive non-verbal cues (eye contact, smile, open posture).
   - Second time: Manager uses negative cues (looking away, crossed arms, frowning).
2. Step 2 (5 minutes): Participants discuss in small groups:
   - How did the manager's non-verbal cues change the employee's response?
   - Which cues made the feedback feel constructive vs. discouraging?
3. Step 3 (5 minutes): Facilitator leads a group discussion:
   - Share observations and connect to workplace scenarios (e.g., presentations, client meetings).
   - Brainstorm 2-3 non-verbal cues to practice daily (e.g., nodding during conversations).

Facilitator Tips

- Choose confident volunteers to avoid discomfort.
- Encourage observers to take notes on specific cues (e.g., "Frowning made the feedback feel harsh").
- Relate to cultural differences if relevant to the group. Illustration: Show a "Non-Verbal Impact" diagram:
  - A central figure with arrows pointing to "Eye Contact," "Posture," "Gestures," and "Facial Expression."
  - Each arrow links to an outcome (e.g., "Eye Contact → Builds Trust").

Actionable Tips

1. Apply the 3C Rule: Ensure all communication is Clear, Concise, and Courteous. Before speaking or writing, ask: "Is my message easy to understand? Brief? Respectful?"
2. Use the SBI Feedback Model: When giving feedback, structure it as:
   - Situation: "During yesterday's meeting…"
   - Behavior: "You interrupted several times…"
   - Impact: "Which made it hard for others to share ideas." Example: "In our team meeting, when you shared your ideas without pausing, it limited others' input. Can we work on balancing participation?"

3. Daily Reflection: Spend 5 minutes at the end of each day reviewing one communication interaction (e.g., a meeting, email, or conversation). Ask:
   - What went well?
   - What could I improve (e.g., tone, clarity, listening)?
   - Write one goal for the next day (e.g., "Pause before responding to questions").
4. Practice Mirroring: In conversations, subtly mirror the other person's body language (e.g., leaning forward if they do) to build rapport. Be natural to avoid seeming artificial.
5. Email Signature Setup: Create a professional email signature (Name, Title, Contact Info) to enhance credibility. Example:
6. Alex Carter
7. Project Manager | ABC Corp
   alex.carter@abccorp.com | (555) 123-4567

Illustration Idea

Create a "Communication Toolkit" infographic:

- A toolbox with icons for:
  - 3C Rule (a checklist).
  - SBI Model (a speech bubble).
  - Daily Reflection (a journal).
  - Mirroring (two figures facing each other).
  - Email Signature (an envelope).
- Caption: "Use these tools daily to elevate your communication."

Real-World Scenarios

To reinforce learning, present these scenarios for discussion or role-play:

1. Scenario 1: Misunderstood Email
   - Context: You send an email requesting a report, but the recipient misinterprets it as a criticism.
   - Task: Rewrite the email to ensure clarity and a positive tone.
   - Discussion: How can tone be conveyed in writing?
2. Scenario 2: Tense Team Meeting
   - Context: During a meeting, a colleague dominates the conversation, and others disengage.

- Task: Role-play how you'd intervene using active listening and non-verbal cues.
- Discussion: How can non-verbal signals shift group dynamics?

3. Scenario 3: Client Presentation
    - Context: You're presenting to a client who seems uninterested.
    - Task: List verbal and non-verbal strategies to re-engage them (e.g., asking questions, smiling).
    - Discussion: How do you adapt communication to a tough audience?

Illustration Idea

For each scenario, create a "Problem vs. Solution" slide:

- Problem: A cartoon of the scenario (e.g., a confused email recipient).
- Solution: A checklist of strategies (e.g., "Clear subject line, Polite tone").

Facilitator's Guide

Preparation

- Materials: Handouts (Listening Checklist, Poor Email Sample, SBI Model), whiteboard, markers, projector for slides.
- Room Setup: Arrange seats in a U-shape for discussion or small tables for group work.
- Slides: Prepare 8-10 slides:
    1. Module Objectives and Why It Matters.
    2. Verbal Communication Triangle.
    3. Body Language Do's and Don'ts.
    4. Before and After Email.
    5. Listening Checklist.
    6. Non-Verbal Impact Diagram.
    7. Communication Toolkit.
    8. Real-World Scenarios.

Delivery Tips

- Engage Early: Start with a quick icebreaker: "Share a time when a communication misunderstanding caused a problem."
- Encourage Participation: Call on quieter participants during debriefs, but avoid putting them on the spot.

- Relate to Audience: Ask participants to share workplace examples (e.g., "How do you communicate with clients vs. colleagues?").
- Manage Time: Stick to the schedule:
  - 10 minutes: Introduction and Key Concepts.
  - 20 minutes: Active Listening Role-Play.
  - 15 minutes: Email Rewrite Challenge.
  - 15 minutes: Non-Verbal Communication Observation.
  - 10 minutes: Actionable Tips and Wrap-Up.
- Handle Resistance: If participants doubt the value of soft skills, share data (e.g., "93% of employers value soft skills as much as technical skills" – LinkedIn, 2019).

Follow-Up

- Assign a post-training task: "For one week, apply the 3C Rule to all emails and reflect on the impact."
- Provide a feedback form to assess the module's effectiveness (e.g., "Rate your confidence in active listening: 1-5")

2

Teamwork and Collaboration

Duration: 60-75 minutes

Objective: Equip participants with the skills to work effectively in diverse teams, fostering trust, clear roles, and constructive conflict resolution to achieve shared goals.

Why It Matters

Teamwork drives innovation, productivity, and workplace morale. Effective collaboration leverages diverse strengths, but poor teamwork can lead to miscommunication, duplicated efforts, or resentment. For example, a team without clear roles might miss deadlines, or unresolved conflicts can erode trust. This module empowers participants to build cohesive, high-performing teams.

Learning Outcomes: By the end of this module, participants will:

1. Understand the principles of trust, role clarity, and conflict resolution in teams.
2. Practice collaborative decision-making and communication in team settings.
3. Develop strategies to strengthen team dynamics and resolve conflicts constructively.

Key Concepts

1. Building Trust

Trust is the foundation of teamwork. It creates a safe environment for sharing ideas and taking risks.

- **Reliability**: Meet deadlines and fulfill commitments. For example, consistently delivering your part of a project builds confidence in your teammates.
- **Respect**: Value diverse perspectives, even when they differ from your own. Acknowledge contributions (e.g., "Great idea, Sarah!").

- **Transparency**: Share challenges or limitations early to avoid surprises. For instance, saying, "I'm struggling with this task—can we brainstorm solutions?" fosters openness.

Illustration Idea

Create a **"Trust Triangle" slide**:

- **Reliability** (base): A calendar with checkmarks, labeled "Deliver on Promises."
- **Respect** (left side): A handshake, labeled "Value All Voices."
- **Transparency** (right side): An open book, labeled "Share Honestly." Caption: "Trust strengthens team bonds."

2. Role Clarity

Clear roles prevent overlap, confusion, and inefficiency.

- **Define Responsibilities**: Ensure each team member knows their tasks and deliverables. For example, in a marketing campaign, one person handles design, another content, and another analytics.
- **Communicate Expectations**: Agree on timelines and quality standards upfront. Use tools like RACI charts (Responsible, Accountable, Consulted, Informed).
- **Flexibility**: Be willing to adjust roles as needs evolve, such as taking on extra tasks during a crunch period.

Illustration Idea

Show a **"RACI Chart Example"**

- Task: Launch Email Campaign.
- Rows: Team members (e.g., Designer, Writer, Manager).
- Columns: Responsible, Accountable, Consulted, Informed.
- Example: Designer (Responsible), Manager (Accountable), Writer (Consulted), Analyst (Informed). Caption: "Clarity prevents chaos."

3. Conflict Resolution

Conflicts are inevitable but can be constructive if handled well.

- **Focus on Issues, Not People**: Address behaviors or outcomes, not personalities. Instead of "You're always late," say, "Late submissions delay our progress."
- **Use "I" Statements**: Express feelings without blame (e.g., "I feel frustrated when meetings start late because it disrupts my schedule").

- **Seek Win-Win Solutions**: Collaborate to find mutually beneficial outcomes. For example, if two team members disagree on a project approach, brainstorm a hybrid solution.

Illustration Idea

Design a **"Conflict Resolution Ladder"**:

- Step 1: "Identify Issue" (a magnifying glass).
- Step 2: "Use 'I' Statements" (a speech bubble).
- Step 3: "Propose Solutions" (a lightbulb).
- Step 4: "Agree and Act" (a handshake). Caption: "Climb from conflict to collaboration."

Activities

Activity 1: Desert Island Scenario (25 minutes)

Objective: Practice collaborative decision-making and role clarity. **Setup**: Divide participants into groups of 4-5. Provide a handout with the scenario and a list of 10 items (e.g., water, rope, matches, tarp). **Scenario**: "Your team is stranded on a desert island Choose 5 items to survive and justify your choices."

Instructions

1. **Step 1 (10 minutes)**: Each group discusses and selects 5 items. Assign roles (e.g., facilitator, note-taker, timekeeper) to ensure clarity.
2. **Step 2 (5 minutes)**: Groups present their choices and reasoning to the larger group.
3. **Debrief (10 minutes)**: Discuss:
   - How did roles help or hinder the process?
   - What conflicts arose, and how were they resolved?
   - How did trust influence decisions?

Facilitator Tips

- Encourage groups to assign roles explicitly.
- Observe dynamics (e.g., who dominates, who stays quiet) and address in debrief.

  Illustration: Handout with a **"Desert Island Map"** showing items scattered, labeled "Work as a team to survive!"

Activity 2: Trust-Building Exercise (15 minutes)

Objective: Build trust through clear communication and reliance. **Setup**: Pair participants; set up a simple obstacle course (e.g., chairs, cones) in the room. Provide blindfolds.

Instructions

1. **Step 1 (7 minutes)**: One partner is blindfolded; the other guides them through the obstacle course using only verbal instructions (e.g., "Step left, slow down"). Switch roles.
2. **Debrief (8 minutes)**: Discuss:
   - How did it feel to rely on your partner?
   - What made instructions effective or unclear?
   - How does this relate to workplace trust?

Facilitator Tips

- Ensure safety (e.g., clear obstacles, slow pace).
- Highlight parallels to workplace reliance (e.g., trusting a colleague's data for a report).

  Illustration: Slide with a **"Trust Pathway"**: A blindfolded figure guided by a partner, labeled "Clear communication builds trust."

Activity 3: Conflict Role-Play (15 minutes)

Objective: Practice resolving conflicts constructively.

Setup: Provide a scenario card (e.g., "Two team members disagree on a project timeline—one wants speed, the other quality"). Pair participants.

Instructions

1. **Step 1 (7 minutes)**: Pairs role-play the scenario, using "I" statements and aiming for a win-win solution.
2. **Step 2 (8 minutes)**: Debrief in small groups:
   - What worked well in resolving the conflict?
   - How did "I" statements change the tone?
   - What challenges arose?

Facilitator Tips

- Provide a script example for hesitant participants.
- Emphasize focusing on solutions, not blame.

  Illustration: Handout with **"Conflict Resolution Cheat Sheet"**

- Step 1: State the issue calmly.
- Step 2: Use "I" statements.
- Step 3: Suggest solutions.
- Step 4: Agree on next steps.

Actionable Tips

1. **Weekly Check-Ins**: Schedule 15-minute team huddles to align on goals, clarify roles, and address concerns.
2. **Acknowledge Contributions**: Publicly recognize team members' efforts (e.g., "Thanks, John, for your detailed analysis").
3. **Conflict Pause**: When tensions rise, take a 5-minute break to cool off before discussing solutions.
4. **Role Mapping**: At the start of a project, create a visual chart of roles and responsibilities to ensure clarity.
5. **Trust Journal**: Reflect weekly on one action you took to build trust (e.g., being transparent about a delay).

Illustration Idea

Create a **"Teamwork Toolkit" infographic**:

- Icons for:
  - Check-Ins (a calendar).
  - Acknowledgment (a thumbs-up).
  - Conflict Pause (a clock).
  - Role Mapping (a chart).
  - Trust Journal (a notebook).

    Caption: "Tools for stronger teams."

Facilitator's Guide

Preparation: Handouts (scenario, RACI chart, cheat sheet), blindfolds, obstacle course items, whiteboard.

Slides: Trust Triangle, RACI Chart, Conflict Resolution Ladder, Teamwork Toolkit.

Delivery Tips

- Start with a question: "What makes a great team?"
- Encourage storytelling (e.g., "Share a time your team succeeded or struggled").

- Manage dominant participants by assigning roles in activities. **Follow-Up**: Assign: "This week, clarify one role or resolve one minor team conflict and report back."

3

Problem-Solving

Duration: 60-75 minutes

Objective: Develop creative and analytical skills to identify, analyze, and resolve workplace challenges effectively.

Why It Matters

Problem-solving is critical for overcoming obstacles, improving processes, and driving innovation. Effective problem-solvers think critically and act decisively, while poor problem-solving leads to delays or ineffective solutions. For example, misdiagnosing a client complaint can escalate issues, while a structured approach resolves it quickly. This module equips participants with practical tools to tackle problems confidently.

Learning Outcomes: By the end of this module, participants will:

1. Understand a structured process for problem-solving (define, generate, evaluate, implement).
2. Practice root cause analysis and brainstorming techniques.
3. Apply problem-solving strategies to real-world scenarios.

Key Concepts

1. Define the Problem

Accurate problem definition prevents wasted effort on symptoms.

- **Ask Questions**: Use "What, Who, When, Where, Why" to clarify the issue. For example, "What's causing project delays?"
- **5 Whys Technique**: Ask "Why?" five times to uncover the root cause. Example: "Why are sales dropping? → Customers aren't engaging. Why? → Marketing isn't targeted."
- **Scope the Problem**: Determine its impact and urgency (e.g., "This affects one team vs. the entire company").

Illustration Idea

Show a **"5 Whys Tree"**:

- A trunk labeled "Problem: Sales Drop."
- Branches with "Why?" questions leading to "Root Cause: Poor Targeting." Caption: "Dig deep to solve the real issue."

2. Generate Solutions

Creative brainstorming produces diverse options.

- **Quantity Over Quality**: Generate many ideas without immediate judgment. For example, brainstorm ways to improve team morale (e.g., team outings, recognition programs).
- **Diverse Input**: Involve team members with different perspectives to spark innovation.
- **Use Tools**: Try mind mapping or SCAMPER (Substitute, Combine, Adapt, Modify, Put to another use, Eliminate, Reverse).

Illustration Idea

Create a **"Mind Map Example"**

- Central node: "Improve Team Morale."
- Branches: "Recognition," "Events," "Flexible Hours," with sub-branches for details.

  Caption: "Map ideas to spark creativity."

3. Evaluate and Implement

Choose the best solution and act on it.

- **Weigh Pros and Cons**: Compare solutions based on feasibility, cost, and impact. For example, a team outing may boost morale but cost more than a recognition program.
- **Test Small**: Pilot solutions to minimize risk (e.g., try a new process for one week).
- **Monitor Results**: Track outcomes and adjust as needed. Use KPIs (e.g., "Did customer complaints decrease by 20%?").

Illustration Idea

Design a **"Decision Matrix"**:

- Rows: Solutions (e.g., Outing, Recognition).
- Columns: Criteria (Cost, Impact, Feasibility).
- Scores: 1-5 for each cell.

  Caption: "Choose wisely with data."

Activities

Activity 1: Case Study Analysis (25 minutes)

Objective: Apply a structured problem-solving process.

Setup: Provide a scenario (e.g., "Client complaints have increased due to slow response times"). Divide into groups of 4-5.

Instructions

1. **Step 1 (10 minutes)**: Groups define the problem, brainstorm solutions, and select one using a decision matrix.
2. **Step 2 (5 minutes)**: Groups present their solution and rationale.
3. **Debrief (10 minutes)**: Discuss:
   - How did defining the problem shape solutions?
   - What tools (e.g., 5 Whys, brainstorming) were most helpful?

Facilitator Tips

- Provide a template for the decision matrix.
- Encourage creative solutions.

  Illustration: Handout with **"Problem-Solving Steps"**: Define, Generate, Evaluate, Implement.

Activity 2: 5 Whys Exercise (15 minutes)

Objective: Practice root cause analysis.

Setup: Provide a problem (e.g., "Project delays are increasing").

Instructions

1. **Step 1 (7 minutes)**: In pairs, ask "Why?" five times to identify the root cause.
2. **Debrief (8 minutes)**: Share findings and discuss:
   - Did the root cause surprise you?
   - How can this method apply to your work?

Facilitator Tips

- Guide pairs to stay focused on one problem.
- Highlight real-world applications (e.g., diagnosing process issues).

  Illustration: Slide with a **"5 Whys Flowchart"**: Problem → Why? → Why? → Root Cause.

Activity 3: SCAMPER Brainstorm (15 minutes)

Objective: Encourage creative solution generation.

Setup: Provide a challenge (e.g., "Improve employee onboarding").

Instructions

1. **Step 1 (7 minutes)**: In small groups, use SCAMPER prompts to brainstorm ideas (e.g., "What can we eliminate from onboarding?").
2. **Debrief (8 minutes)**: Share ideas and discuss:
    - Which SCAMPER prompt sparked the best ideas?
    - How can creativity improve problem-solving?

Facilitator Tips

- Provide a SCAMPER handout with prompts.
- Encourage wild ideas to stretch thinking.

  Illustration: Handout with **"SCAMPER Wheel"**: Segments labeled Substitute, Combine, etc.

Actionable Tips

1. **Problem Journal**: Log challenges and solutions weekly to track patterns.
2. **Break Reset**: When stuck, take a 10-minute walk to refresh perspective.
3. **Team Input**: Always seek at least one colleague's perspective before finalizing a solution.
4. **Pilot Test**: Test solutions on a small scale before full rollout.
5. **Celebrate Wins**: Acknowledge successful solutions to boost confidence (e.g., "Our new process cut delays by 20%!").

Illustration Idea

"Problem-Solving Toolkit" infographic

- Icons: Journal, Break, Team Input, Pilot, Celebration.

  Caption: "Solve smarter, not harder."

Facilitator's Guide

Preparation: Handouts (scenario, SCAMPER prompts, decision matrix), whiteboard.

Slides: 5 Whys Tree, Mind Map, Decision Matrix, Toolkit.

Delivery Tips

- Start with a question: “What’s a problem you solved recently?”
- Use humor to lighten complex concepts (e.g., “Ever solve the mystery of the missing office coffee?”).

  Follow-Up: Assign: “Apply the 5 Whys to one work challenge this week.”

4

Time Management

Duration: 60-75 minutes

Objective: Master techniques to prioritize tasks, meet deadlines, and reduce stress for improved productivity and work-life balance.

Why It Matters

Effective time management ensures focus on high-impact tasks, reduces procrastination, and prevents burnout. Poor time management leads to missed deadlines, stress, and lower quality work. For example, spending hours on emails instead of strategic planning can derail priorities. This module provides tools to optimize time usage.

Learning Outcomes: By the end of this module, participants will:

1. Understand prioritization and planning techniques (e.g., Eisenhower Matrix, Pomodoro).
2. Practice strategies to minimize distractions and delegate effectively.
3. Create a personalized time management plan.

Key Concepts

1. Prioritization

Focus on what matters most.

- **Eisenhower Matrix**: Categorize tasks by urgency and importance:
  - Urgent & Important: Do immediately (e.g., client crisis).
  - Important, Not Urgent: Schedule (e.g., long-term planning).
  - Urgent, Not Important: Delegate (e.g., routine emails).
  - Neither: Eliminate (e.g., unnecessary meetings).
- **80/20 Rule**: 20% of tasks produce 80% of results. Identify high-impact tasks daily.
- **Say No**: Politely decline low-priority requests (e.g., “I’d love to help, but my current priorities are X and Y”).

Illustration Idea

Show an **"Eisenhower Matrix"**

- 2x2 grid with quadrants labeled Do, Schedule, Delegate, Eliminate.
- Example tasks in each (e.g., "Client deadline" in Do).

  Caption: "Prioritize to maximize impact."

2. Planning

Break tasks into manageable steps.

- **Daily Planning**: Spend 5 minutes each morning listing top 3 priorities.
- **Task Chunking**: Divide large projects into smaller tasks (e.g., "Write report" becomes "Outline, Draft, Edit").
- **Tools**: Use calendars (Google Calendar) or apps (Trello, Todoist) to track deadlines.

Illustration Idea

Create a **"Task Breakdown Example"**

- Project: "Launch Campaign."
- Steps: Research, Design, Review, Publish.
- Deadlines next to each step.

  Caption: "Small steps lead to big wins."

3. Avoiding Distractions

Stay focused in a busy world.

- **Time Blocking**: Reserve specific times for tasks (e.g., 9-10 AM for emails).
- **Minimize Interruptions**: Silence notifications, use "Do Not Disturb" modes, or work in quiet spaces.
- **Delegation**: Assign routine tasks to others when possible (e.g., "Can you handle the data entry?").

Illustration Idea

Design a **"Distraction Shield"**:

- A shield with sections: Time Blocking, Notifications Off, Delegation. Caption: "Protect your focus."

Activities

Activity 1: Eisenhower Matrix Workshop (20 minutes)

Objective: Practice prioritizing tasks.

Setup: Provide a list of 10 tasks (e.g., "Answer emails," "Prepare presentation"). Hand out a blank Eisenhower Matrix.

Instructions

1. **Step 1 (7 minutes)**: Individually, categorize tasks into the matrix.
2. **Step 2 (5 minutes)**: In pairs, compare and discuss choices.
3. **Debrief (8 minutes)**: Discuss:
   - How did prioritization change your approach?
   - What tasks were hard to categorize?

Facilitator Tips

- Provide a sample matrix for reference.
- Highlight delegation as a key strategy.

  Illustration: Handout with a **blank Eisenhower Matrix**.

Activity 2: Time Audit (15 minutes)

Objective: Identify time wasters.

Setup: Ask participants to track their time for one day prior to the session (or provide a sample log).

Instructions

1. **Step 1 (7 minutes)**: In pairs, analyze the log to identify effective vs. wasted time (e.g., "30 minutes on social media").
2. **Debrief (8 minutes)**: Share insights and discuss:
   - What surprised you about your time use?
   - What's one change you'll make?

Facilitator Tips

- Offer a template log (e.g., hourly breakdown).
- Emphasize small changes (e.g., "Cut email time by 10 minutes"). **Illustration**: Slide with a **"Time Pie Chart"**: Segments for Work, Emails, Distractions.

Activity 3: Pomodoro Simulation (15 minutes)

Objective: Experience focused work intervals.

Setup: Provide a simple task (e.g., brainstorm ideas for a project). Set a timer.

Instructions

1. **Step 1 (7 minutes)**: Work for 5 minutes, take a 1-minute break, then work 5 more minutes.
2. **Debrief (8 minutes)**: Discuss:
    - How did short bursts affect focus?
    - Could you use Pomodoro daily?

Facilitator Tips

- Keep the task light to focus on the technique.
- Explain scaling to 25-minute intervals.

  Illustration: Slide with a **"Pomodoro Clock"**: 5-minute work, 1-minute break.

Actionable Tips

1. **Morning Plan**: Start each day with a 5-minute priority list.
2. **Pomodoro Practice**: Use 25-minute work sessions for deep focus.
3. **Delegate Smart**: Identify one task weekly to delegate.
4. **Notification Off**: Silence non-essential alerts during work hours.
5. **Weekly Review**: Reflect on time management wins and challenges.

Illustration Idea

"Time Management Toolkit" infographic

- Icons: Morning Plan, Pomodoro, Delegation, Notifications, Review. Caption: "Own your time."

Facilitator's Guide

Preparation: Handouts (task list, matrix, time log), timer, whiteboard.

Slides: Eisenhower Matrix, Task Breakdown, Distraction Shield, Toolkit.

Delivery Tips

- Start with: "What's your biggest time management struggle?"
- Share a relatable example (e.g., "I once spent an hour on emails instead of a key task").

  Follow-Up: Assign: "Try Pomodoro for one task this week."

5

Adaptability

Duration: 60-75 minutes

Objective: Build resilience and flexibility to thrive in changing environments, embracing new challenges and opportunities.

Why It Matters

In today's fast-paced world, adaptability ensures you can handle disruptions, learn new skills, and stay relevant. Resistance to change leads to stress and missed opportunities. For example, adapting to a new software tool can boost efficiency, while resisting it can hinder performance. This module equips participants to embrace change confidently.

Learning Outcomes: By the end of this module, participants will:

1. Understand the importance of a growth mindset and resilience.
2. Practice strategies to cope with change and learn new skills.
3. Develop a personal adaptability plan.

Key Concepts

1. Growth Mindset

View challenges as opportunities to grow.

- **Embrace Learning**: See setbacks as feedback (e.g., "This failed project taught me better planning").
- **Stay Curious**: Ask questions and explore new ideas (e.g., "How can this new process improve my work?").
- **Seek Feedback**: Use input to improve, even if it's uncomfortable.

Illustration Idea

Show a **"Mindset Shift"**:

- Fixed Mindset: A closed door labeled "I can't do this."
- Growth Mindset: An open door labeled "I'll learn how."

  Caption: "Choose growth over fear."

2. Skill Development

Stay relevant by building new competencies.

- **Continuous Learning**: Dedicate time to learning (e.g., online courses, workshops).
- **Cross-Training**: Learn adjacent roles to increase versatility (e.g., a marketer learning basic analytics).
- **Experimentation**: Try new approaches in low-risk settings (e.g., test a new meeting format).

Illustration Idea

Create a **"Skill Tree"**:

- Trunk: "Core Skills."
- Branches: "New Tools," "Cross-Training," "Experiments."

  Caption: "Grow your skills to adapt."

3. Coping with Change

Manage stress and uncertainty effectively.

- **Control Focus**: Focus on what you can influence (e.g., your response, not external events).
- **Stress Management**: Use techniques like deep breathing or journaling to stay calm.
- **Small Steps**: Break change into manageable actions (e.g., learn one feature of a new tool daily).

Illustration Idea

Design a **"Change Wave"**:

- A wave with stages: Shock, Resistance, Acceptance, Action.
- Arrows showing "Focus," "Breathe," "Act" to ride the wave.

  Caption: "Surf change with resilience."

Activities

Activity 1: Change Simulation (25 minutes)

Objective: Practice adapting to change.

Setup: Provide a scenario (e.g., "Your team must adopt a new software tool"). Divide into groups of 4-5.

Instructions

1. **Step 1 (10 minutes)**: Groups list challenges, opportunities, and an action plan to adapt.
2. **Step 2 (5 minutes)**: Present plans to the group.
3. **Debrief (10 minutes)**: Discuss:
   - How did you feel about the change?
   - What strategies made adaptation easier?

Facilitator Tips

- Encourage emotional honesty in debrief.
- Highlight proactive strategies.

  Illustration: Handout with **"Change Plan Template"**: Challenges, Opportunities, Actions.

Activity 2: Growth Mindset Reflection (15 minutes)

Objective: Reframe setbacks as learning opportunities.

Setup: Provide paper or a digital form.

Instructions

1. **Step 1 (7 minutes)**: Write about a past failure and what you learned (e.g., "I missed a deadline but learned to plan better").
2. **Debrief (8 minutes)**: Share in pairs and discuss:
   - How did reframing change your perspective?
   - How can you apply this mindset daily?

Facilitator Tips

- Create a safe space for sharing.
- Emphasize learning, not judgment.

  Illustration: Slide with **"Failure to Growth"**: A broken arrow transforming into a strong one.

Activity 3: Skill-Building Challenge (15 minutes)

Objective: Commit to learning a new skill.

Setup: Provide a list of micro-skills (e.g., "Learn one Excel function," "Try a new meeting icebreaker").

Instructions

1. **Step 1 (7 minutes)**: Individually, choose one skill and outline a 1-week plan to learn it.

2. **Debrief (8 minutes)**: Share plans and discuss:
   - Why did you choose this skill?
   - How will it help you adapt?

Facilitator Tips

- Encourage achievable goals.
- Suggest resources (e.g., YouTube tutorials).
  Illustration: Handout with **"Skill Plan"**: Skill, Steps, Timeline.

Actionable Tips

1. **Weekly Learning**: Dedicate 1 hour to a new skill or tool.
2. **Change Question**: When facing change, ask, "What's one step I can take today?"
3. **Mindfulness Pause**: Practice 1-minute deep breathing during stress.
4. **Feedback Loop**: Seek feedback monthly to identify growth areas.
5. **Adaptability Log**: Track one change you navigated each week.

Illustration Idea

"Adaptability Toolkit" infographic:

- Icons: Learning, Question, Mindfulness, Feedback, Log.
  Caption: "Thrive in any storm."

Facilitator's Guide

Preparation: Handouts (scenario, skill list, plan template), paper.

Slides: Mindset Shift, Skill Tree, Change Wave, Toolkit.

Delivery Tips

- Start with: "How do you handle unexpected changes?"
- Share a personal change story to build rapport.
  Follow-Up: Assign: "Learn one micro-skill this week."

6

Emotional Intelligence (EQ)

Duration: 60-75 minutes

Objective: Enhance self-awareness, empathy, and relationship management to build stronger workplace connections and leadership skills.

Why It Matters

Emotional intelligence drives effective collaboration, leadership, and conflict resolution. High EQ creates positive workplace cultures, while low EQ can lead to misunderstandings or disengagement. For example, an empathetic response to a stressed colleague builds trust, while a dismissive one erodes it. This module equips participants to manage emotions and relationships effectively.

Learning Outcomes: By the end of this module, participants will:

1. Understand the four components of EQ: self-awareness, self-regulation, empathy, relationship management.
2. Practice empathetic listening and emotional regulation.
3. Develop strategies to strengthen interpersonal relationships.

Key Concepts

1. Self-Awareness

Recognize and understand your emotions.

- **Identify Triggers**: Notice what sparks strong emotions (e.g., tight deadlines cause stress).
- **Reflect Regularly**: Journal or pause to assess your emotional state.
- **Impact Awareness**: Understand how your emotions affect others (e.g., snapping under pressure demotivates a team).

Illustration Idea

Show a **"Self-Awareness Mirror"**:

- A mirror reflecting emotions (happy, stressed).
- Arrows to "Triggers" and "Impact."

  Caption: "See yourself clearly."

2. Self-Regulation

Manage emotions constructively.

- **Pause Before Reacting**: Take a breath to avoid impulsive responses (e.g., don't send an angry email immediately).
- **Positive Self-Talk**: Reframe challenges (e.g., "This is tough, but I can handle it").
- **Stress Relief**: Use quick techniques like stretching or a walk to reset.

Illustration Idea

Create a **"Regulation Dial"**:

- A dial with settings: Pause, Self-Talk, Stress Relief.

  Caption: "Turn down emotional heat."

3. Empathy

Understand and share others' feelings.

- **Active Listening**: Listen to understand, not respond (e.g., nod, paraphrase).
- **Validate Feelings**: Acknowledge emotions (e.g., "I can see why you're frustrated").
- **Perspective-Taking**: Imagine others' viewpoints (e.g., "How might a new hire feel in this meeting?").

Illustration Idea

Design an **"Empathy Bridge"**:

- Two figures connected by a bridge labeled "Listen, Validate, Understand." Caption: "Connect through empathy."

4. Relationship Management

Build and maintain strong connections.

- **Rapport**: Use consistent, respectful interactions (e.g., regular checkins).
- **Conflict Navigation**: Address issues collaboratively (e.g., "Let's find a solution that works for both of us").
- **Positive Reinforcement**: Offer specific praise (e.g., "Your creativity really moved this project forward").

Illustration Idea

Show a "Relationship Garden"

- Plants labeled Rapport, Conflict Navigation, Praise.
  Caption: "Nurture strong bonds."

Activities

Activity 1: Empathy Role-Play (20 minutes)

Objective: Practice empathetic listening.

Setup: Pair participants; provide a scenario (e.g., "A colleague is frustrated about workload").

Instructions

1. **Step 1 (10 minutes)**: Person A shares the issue; Person B listens empathetically (no advice, just validation). Switch roles.
2. **Debrief (10 minutes)**: Discuss:
   - How did empathy affect the conversation?
   - What was challenging about not giving advice?

Facilitator Tips

- Model empathetic listening first.
- Encourage non-verbal cues (e.g., nodding).
  Illustration: Handout with **"Empathy Checklist"**: Listen, Validate, Reflect.

Activity 2: Emotion Journal (15 minutes)

Objective: Build self-awareness.

Setup: Provide paper or a digital form.

Instructions

1. **Step 1 (7 minutes)**: Write about one emotional reaction from the past week (trigger, response, outcome).
2. **Debrief (8 minutes)**: Share in small groups:
   - What patterns did you notice?
   - How can you regulate better next time?

Facilitator Tips

- Ensure confidentiality.
- Suggest regulation strategies (e.g., pausing).
  Illustration: Slide with **"Emotion Cycle"**: Trigger → Reaction → Outcome.

Activity 3: Relationship-Building Challenge (15 minutes)

Objective: Strengthen workplace connections.

Setup: Provide a list of actions (e.g., "Give specific praise," "Check in with a colleague").

Instructions

1. **Step 1 (7 minutes)**: Choose one action to try this week and plan how to do it.
2. **Debrief (8 minutes)**: Share plans and discuss:
   - Why did you choose this action?
   - How will it improve relationships?

Facilitator Tips

- Encourage small, achievable actions.
- Highlight long-term benefits.

  Illustration: Handout with **"Relationship Actions"**: Praise, Check-In, Collaborate.

Actionable Tips

1. **Daily Reflection**: Spend 5 minutes noting emotions and triggers.
2. **2-Second Pause**: Hesitate before responding in tense moments.
3. **Empathy Practice**: Validate one person's feelings daily.
4. **Praise Habit**: Offer specific praise weekly.
5. **Relationship Check-In**: Connect with one colleague weekly.

Illustration Idea

"EQ Toolkit" infographic

- Icons: Reflection, Pause, Empathy, Praise, Check-In.

  Caption: "Build stronger connections."

Facilitator's Guide

Preparation: Handouts (scenario, checklist, action list), paper.

Slides: Self-Awareness Mirror, Regulation Dial, Empathy Bridge, Relationship Garden, Toolkit.

Delivery Tips

- Start with: "What's a time someone's empathy made a difference for you?"

- Create a safe space for emotional discussions.

  Follow-Up: Assign: "Try one empathy action this week."

Conclusion

As we conclude this Training Manual on Soft Skills, reflect on the transformative power of the skills you've explored: effective communication, teamwork and collaboration, problem-solving, time management, adaptability, and emotional intelligence. These competencies are not just tools for workplace success—they are the foundation for building meaningful relationships, driving innovation, and navigating the complexities of modern professional life. By mastering these skills, you position yourself as a confident, collaborative, and resilient leader, capable of thriving in any environment.

This manual has provided a structured, practical framework to develop and refine these essential soft skills. Through engaging activities, real-world scenarios, and actionable strategies, you've gained insights into how small, intentional changes can yield significant results. Whether it's crafting a clearer email, resolving a team conflict, prioritizing high-impact tasks, embracing change, or responding with empathy, each step you take strengthens your ability to connect, contribute, and grow.

Key Takeaways

- Soft skills are universal: They enhance every role, industry, and interaction, making you more effective and adaptable.
- Practice makes progress: Consistent application and reflection are key to turning these skills into habits.
- Impact is cumulative: Small improvements in communication, collaboration, or time management compound over time, leading to lasting personal and professional growth.

Your Next Steps

1. Create a 30-Day Action Plan: Select one skill from each module to focus on over the next month. For example, practice active listening (Module 1) one week, clarify team roles (Module 2) the next, and so on. Track your progress in a journal or with a colleague.
2. Seek Feedback: Engage with peers, managers, or mentors to gain insights into your strengths and areas for growth. Ask specific questions like, "How clear was my presentation?" or "How can I contribute more effectively to our team?"

3. Revisit and Reflect: Return to this manual periodically to refresh your skills, try new activities, or adapt strategies to new challenges. Use the provided resources (books, online courses, apps) to deepen your learning.
4. Share Your Knowledge: Teach a colleague a soft skills tip or lead a team discussion on collaboration. Sharing reinforces your learning and strengthens your workplace culture.

The journey to mastering soft skills is ongoing, but every effort you invest brings you closer to becoming a more impactful professional and a more empathetic human being. Embrace the process, celebrate your progress, and continue to grow with curiosity and confidence. You have the tools—now go make a difference.